Who F**ted?

AURA

Every effort has been made to trace the copyright holders of the photographs featured.
Any enquiries regarding their reproduction should be sent to the publishers:
SJG Publishing, Markyate, Hertfordshire AL3 8LE.

This edition published in 2003 by
Advanced Marketing (UK) Ltd, Bicester, Oxfordshire
Copyright ©2003 Susanna Geoghegan
All rights reserved
Designed by Milestone Design
Text supplied by Peter Wilkinson
Printed in China by Imago
ISBN 1903938384

"Mr Darcy ~

a most impressive symphony

in B flat"

!

"If I uncross my legs, we are going to clear the Dress Circle"

"Forgive her sir ~
Sue knows not wot Sue
has done!"

"I recommend a rose
for that condition & you won't
need a vase!"

"I don't know much about children but this one needs a cork!"

"You sir, have done a trouser cough and don't deny it!"

"Now Mr Windy, you were meant to sweep me off my feet!"

"One more of those love and they are going to have to lower the safety curtain!"

"Tarquin,
was that a bum note?"

"Sir Henry,
have you whistled in
your Y-fronts?"

"Yeah...

cotton picking beans!"

26

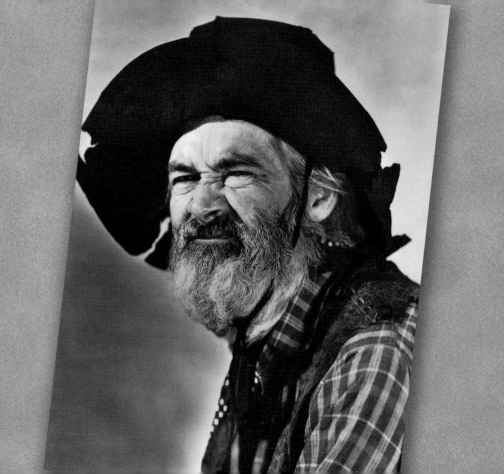

"Well who else
could have done it?"

"Percy proved it was
not only the fast bowler who
had an outstanding
follow-through"

"That's the last time we feed him tripe, eggs and cabbage!"

"I definitely saw
your epaulettes flutter!"

"That's the plumbing my dear!"

✱ "I believe there's a commotion on your poop-deck, sir!" !

"I think that may well rust my chain mail!"

"Your top hat is fine, but your tails are wagging!"

"Beg pardon, ~
Doc's put me on a
high-fibre diet!"

"It must
be the Danish bacon!"

"Watch this!
Double salco ~ Wind assisted"

"...and what does madame do for an encore?"

"This is a clean town, mister. We don't need your sort with your repeaters and your six-shooters!"

give it time!

"So it was you who had the last prunes and custard, you old rascal!"

"That one has brought a bit of colour to your cheeks!"

"Cecil, I think
you've dropped more than
your monocle!"

"I bet they
don't put up with that at
the RSC!"

"Percival, am I mistaken or have you floated an air biscuit?"